BEYOND THE BITCOIN HYPE

AN INTRODUCTION TO BITCOIN & WHY IT WILL FAIL

MARC NOVUS

Copyright © 2014 Marc Novus

All rights reserved.

Beyond the Bitcoin Hype: An Introduction to Bitcoin and Why It Will Fail is not approved, endorsed, sponsored, or otherwise affiliated with any of the organizations, companies, corporations, groups, or parties referenced in this book. Any trademarks, service marks, product names, or named features are assumed to be the property of their respective owners and are used only for reference. This book does not convey nor is a substitute for professional legal, financial, or investment advice. This book is published solely for informational and educational purposes and it does not form the basis of any contract or commitment. Information in this book does not constitute a recommendation to buy, sell, or hold bitcoins, or any security, financial product, or instrument. The author is not liable for damages caused by actions taken as a result of the information in this book.

Originally published as an e-book February, 2014.

Cover design by Marc Novus.

ISBN: 1496046862
ISBN-13: 978-1496046864

DEDICATION

For my mother and my father and my friends.

CONTENTS

	Acknowledgments	i
1	Why This Book?	1
2	What Are Bitcoins? Why Should I Use Them?	3
3	Main Challenges to Bitcoin Overview	14
4	Hurdles to Acceptance	16
5	Deflation, Hoarding, and the Concentration of Ownership	21
6	Regulation and Control	26
7	The 51% Attack	31
8	Conclusion	33
9	Appendix A: Supplement on Mining	37
10	Topics Omitted	44
11	Further Reading or Information	45
12	References	46
13	About the Author	51

ACKNOWLEDGMENTS

Thank you to Mr. D. for the informative and stimulating conversations we had on all the topics of this book – from the computer background to the economics and the philosophy. Your encouragement and support is much appreciated. Thank you to Mr. O. and Mrs. M. for suggesting I take this path. Thank you to Mr. P. for the proof of concept.

1 - WHY THIS BOOK?

This book is an accessible guide to Bitcoin and the most significant challenges it's facing and will face in the time to come. If you're curious about Bitcoin but don't know where to start reading, this book is for you. If you're considering using Bitcoin as a consumer or accepting it as a vendor, this book will help you decide. You'll have a better understanding of the deeper issues at play when it's in the news. You'll have a base knowledge of the key debates so that you don't get carried away by the hype. You'll know what people are talking about when they talk about Bitcoin, and more. Information, discussion, and debate about these challenges and issues are inconveniently scattered across the Internet. They usually assume a familiarity with Bitcoin that's difficult for the non-technical reader to pick up from a single source.

Maybe you've seen the sensationalist headlines and stories about Bitcoin, proclaiming its glorious success or comical failure – sometimes even in the same article. Reading those articles, you don't get a sense of what's at the heart of Bitcoin. Grasping what Bitcoin is can be confusing enough for people. It doesn't help that the more fundamental topics are ignored, resulting in a shallow and flashy treatment. There's much in the way of entertaining narratives and manufactured controversy. And there's much in the way of empty praise or criticism. But there's little in the way of analysis and thoughtful commentary aimed at a general audience. Gathering all the information needed to create your own stance is time consuming without an introductory guide. As we are soon likely to see the rise of other digital currencies, becoming familiar with Bitcoin can assist in understanding the imminent changes in this landscape. Similar ideas and challenges are sure to surface again. There's no escaping them as the scope of our rights to privacy and freedom in the digital world are increasingly questioned (consider the recent news about the NSA surveillance controversy).

Introducing Bitcoin as an "open source, peer to peer, decentralized cryptocurrency" is bound to alienate readers and already assumes knowledge that is in no way commonplace. There's a web of concepts and arguments that need to be learned first for that definition to really have meaning for a reader. This book can provide that groundwork. I aim to give a clear introduction to Bitcoin, and by doing so, provide a gateway into other interesting discussions and topics. Without a clear and honest explanation of the main issues, opportunities, and limitations, progress will be limited. We'll be starting from the beginning every time Bitcoin is a talking point, rehashing the same pros and cons and getting nowhere.

While this print-version was being prepared, multiple online exchanges (places where Bitcoins are bought and sold in established currencies) were hacked or shut down. Among them was the most well-known exchange, Mt.Gox, based in Tokyo, Japan. These rapid developments give even more reason to learn the fundamental challenges Bitcoin faces. For book updates and commentary, visit the author's blog at http://marcnovus.tumblr.com/.

Marc Novus, Berlin, March 2014

2 - WHAT ARE BITCOINS AND WHY SHOULD I USE THEM?

Bitcoin was designed and created by a person or group of persons under the pseudonym Satoshi Nakamoto. The essence of the Bitcoin system is described in Nakamoto's 2008 paper "Bitcoin: A Peer-to-Peer Electronic Cash System." In the paper, the possibility of "a system for electronic transactions without relying on trust" is shown. In the Bitcoin system, a collection of rules and steps are followed by computer software to ensure transactions between users are properly processed and are valid. Relying upon the Bitcoin system's rules and steps, two willing parties can have direct transactions with each other without the need for a trusted third party (such as a financial institution that will mediate disputes). However, these rules and steps can be examined by anyone because Bitcoin is open source. Anyone can look at the software code and no single party has an exclusive claim on how the software is developed. Perhaps this seems a bit off-putting since Bitcoin can be used to transfer lots of money. But its open source nature means important changes can be rapidly made to respond to user needs in a transparent manner. It allows for greater collaboration that hopefully improves the overall quality and security of the software and network (although there is a core group of developers working on Bitcoin). The Bitcoin network debuted in 2009 and has been functional since.

If that explanation of Bitcoin was too abstract, it's easier to begin with how Bitcoin is used in an everyday context and the unique qualities and advantages it's considered to have. Information and abstract explanations will be gradually introduced to fill in the blanks. However, if you're looking for the quickest introduction, the end of this chapter has a brief summary of Bitcoin and its supposed advantages. It provides enough context for the rest of the chapters. As a convention for this book, "Bitcoin" capitalized refers to the technology, protocol, and network, whereas "bitcoin" or "bitcoins" refer to the currency itself. In other words, interpret "Bitcoin" as the entire system, and "bitcoin" as the specific 'coins' used in transactions.

Think of bitcoins as a kind of electronic cash. You can send your bitcoins through the Internet to another party. For example, you can purchase goods or services from merchants who accept bitcoin as payment instead of using an online credit card service or transferring the funds through your bank. But why would someone use Bitcoin in that case? Credit card or wire transfers are already used all the time and meet many needs.

For one, transactions can generally be processed with little to no transaction fees. Credit card fees affect customers because merchants may wish to adapt their prices to meet the charges they must pay for using the payment system. Since transaction fees are low in Bitcoin, small casual transactions are feasible, because otherwise, the transaction fees would cost more than the revenue earned from selling something at a low-price

Bitcoin transactions only require a user to have an Internet connection, a computer or mobile device, and free computer software. This allows merchants and customers to connect who might be priced out of using credit card payment systems or who live in areas where the infrastructure to support these systems is lacking. Bitcoins can be quickly transferred at any time between users across the world and become available for use almost immediately after. Bank accounts and personal information aren't required, nor are other various related services and intermediary parties.

A Bitcoin address is the only *information* needed for you to send, receive, or store bitcoins. It is similar to an email address, and you can imagine the convenience in transferring bitcoins as being similar to your experience sending emails. A Bitcoin address is an identifier of 27-34 letters and numbers, for example: *31uEbMgunupShBVTewXjtqbBv5MndwfXhb*. That might seem like a rather strange and complicated address. This is because the address is generated by cryptographic methods. Cryptography is the practice of securing communications (keeping its integrity and confidentiality) in the presence of third parties and through exchange across networks. The process involves substantial mathematics, but it is all handled by the Bitcoin "wallet" software, which stores addresses for use.

The relative straight-forwardness of sending bitcoins is due to Bitcoin's peer-to-peer payment network. Peer-to-peer means you as a user in the Bitcoin network interact directly with other users. You are one point of connection, among many other points of connection (other "peers"), that supply and obtain resources from each other. This is in contrast to relying upon only a few central providers or authorities that provide access to resources to a multitude of peers. In other words, a bank is not required as a party to mediate, verify, or confirm transactions. Rather, transactions are managed collectively by the Bitcoin network.

All confirmed transactions are included on what is

called the block chain. The entire Bitcoin network shares the block chain, which is a shared public ledger of all Bitcoin transactions. It is a transaction database that can be viewed by anyone. However, nothing personally identifiable is revealed (e.g., information showing that John Smith, living at 123 Fake Street from San Francisco, USA purchased a t-shirt from Paul's online store with 5 bitcoins). Instead, Bitcoin addresses are used in transactions. As a security measure, users are strongly advised not to use the same public addresses for different transactions. Again, the Bitcoin software makes the creation of new addresses manageable.

The block chain allows for transparency in Bitcoin transactions and the activities of the Bitcoin network. You can view the latest transactions happening around the world or look back to transactions from Bitcoin's early days using a block chain web browser, such as "BlockChain.info". Using such a browser, you can view the public addresses of parties in transactions (those long strings of letters and numbers), the amount of bitcoins sent (with the option to see how much that converts to US dollars or other currencies), and the date/time of the transactions, among other information.

The block chain is made out of many blocks, and each block is a record of a number of Bitcoin transactions. If we imagine the block chain as a ledger, imagine each block as a page in that ledger. But new blocks are not automatically added to the block chain. A new block can contain records of recent transactions that have not been yet submitted to the Bitcoin network. That's not to say the transactions that were recorded on the block can be changed or reversed right then and there. It's just that they haven't been 'locked in' yet.

Blocks are submitted to the Bitcoin network through a process called mining. Mining is basically the solving of difficult math problems by computers. The information for the problems is contained in each block. Once these problems are solved, a block is locked into the block chain. The truth about mining is more complicated, but the explanation that follows is sufficient for the discussions in this book. For a more in-depth explanation that also includes information about the block chain, how transactions are included and verified in mining, and transaction fees, see Appendix A of this book. The chapter on the 51% attack also contains information that slightly complicates this picture.

Mining is a very resource-intensive process. So resource-intensive, in fact, that specialty hardware for the purpose of mining is used by miners (people who participate in mining). There is no restriction on who can become a miner. Yet working alone as a single miner to solve problems, even with specialty hardware (put together as mining rigs), is time consuming. Miners often work together as teams called mining pools to combine their computing power. "But what do miners get out of it?" you might wonder.

Miners or pools of miners who successfully solve the problems are awarded bitcoins. And it's through mining that new bitcoin is introduced into the network. In the case of pooled mining, a steadier but smaller income is traded for the larger but erratic rewards of solo mining. One block is solved every ten minutes. Right now, twenty-five bitcoins are awarded per solved block, but this number will steadily decrease over time so that the number of bitcoins in existence won't exceed twenty-one million. The rate at which bitcoin is awarded approximates the rate at which commodities like gold are mined.

In summary, mining is important for the generation of blocks and maintaining the block chain (something similar to a shared public ledger for the whole network). But as you can see, there's no central authority that issues bitcoins. It is through the decentralized process of block creation through mining that new bitcoins are created.

The lack of a central authority is one of the more

contentious points, but it's worth mentioning because it's included by supporters as one of Bitcoin's advantages. Bitcoin supporters argue in favor of the predictability Bitcoin has over other currencies that depend on central authorities. Users of Bitcoin don't have to place their trust upon a central authority that doesn't necessarily have the users' interests in mind, and may have its own agenda and motivations. Users can also lack confidence in a central authority and its currency because of a history of default, inflation, unstable performance, and a general concern over the possible manipulation of the currency's value. Bitcoin users don't have to trust any central authority or any institution because Bitcoin's security is based on strong cryptographic methods which people can investigate and learn about for themselves. How the Bitcoin network functions is not a secret that is guarded by any authority. Transferring bitcoins, creating bitcoins, and other bitcoin activities rely on cryptography, certain protocols (digital rules for transmitting data between computers), and a network of users. But those activities don't rely on one body, agent, authority, or institution.

The finite supply of bitcoins is another contentious point. The creation of bitcoins slowly decreases every year until 2140, when twenty-one million bitcoins are in existence. Once that predetermined number is reached, no more will be created. However, 99% of all bitcoins will be created by 2032. This scarcity is fuelling the rapidly rising or falling value of Bitcoin when compared to the US dollar as Bitcoin grows. The value of Bitcoin is not pegged to any other currency or is not stabilized to remain within a certain range by any group. The value of one bitcoin compared to one US dollar is what people are willing to pay for bitcoins, and their belief in the likelihood of Bitcoin's value rising. Critics point to the finite supply of Bitcoin as a fatal flaw that leads to dire economic consequences. Essentially the argument is that this feature of Bitcoin entails that it will never actually be spent as it would be more profitable to hold onto Bitcoins and sell them in the indefinite future. Bitcoin supporters criticize this view, challenging its assumptions on the nature of spending money on goods as well its associated economic beliefs. Their view is that a finite supply of bitcoins is advantageous to society because of how a finite currency affects prices and savings, as well as how it incentivizes long term investments. Support for Bitcoin's finite monetary supply is also closely tied to arguments against a central authority that can determine monetary policy (e.g., by issuing new currency). Central authorities might be argued against on political or ethical grounds, by questioning their rights to rule, as well as economic grounds, by arguing that they are inefficient or worsen the prospects of agents.

The market value of one bitcoin compared to one US dollar has risen quite rapidly in late 2013, peaking around $1200 early in December, after spending most of the year before November valued below $200. Later in December, the value fell below $500 after the Chinese government announced it was restricting Bitcoin-Yuan trade.

The fluctuation in value has made some people critical of Bitcoin's purpose as a currency (this issue is tied to the finite supply issue). It's argued that the stability in value isn't there. Instead of Bitcoin being like electronic cash, as I initially described it in the chapter, Bitcoin's commodity or speculative asset nature is stressed, particularly as a comparison to gold. This can be an advantage for certain users of Bitcoin, who may profit from speculating on Bitcoin's value. There was much money to be made if you had bought bitcoin in 2009 and then sold it in November 2013. However, the comparison with gold breaks down in certain respects, such as portability or its utility. But the greater question is whether Bitcoin is better treated as something for speculation or trading, rather than a currency with a long term future that people are comfortable integrating into their daily use.

Bitcoin can be exchanged with currencies at online Bitcoin exchanges. The most popular currency exchange was Mt.Gox (called "Mount Gox"), based in Tokyo, Japan. It was hacked and shut down in February 2014. Online exchanges are based in cities around the world, differing in options for adding and withdrawing funds as well as privacy and security features. However, there are other methods of buying bitcoins than through online exchanges. There are also ways for people to buy bitcoins in person, using websites that connect buyers and sellers in the same city.

As we've nearly reached the end of the chapter, you still might be wondering, "What is Bitcoin, really?" The difficulty in answering that question lies in all the related features of the Bitcoin network and concepts you've encountered so far. A simpler answer will now make sense, whereas before it would likely have seemed to be a group of unfamiliar terms thrown together.

A bitcoin, as in one that you spend, accept, or sell, is just a number. It's an entry in a public ledger (i.e., the block chain) showing that one address can spend a certain number of bitcoins. Once a bitcoin is spent, a message is signed by an address, proving that the address is the one in control of the bitcoin. The message states that the address is reducing their number of bitcoins by a certain amount and adding it to a different address. This change in values is reflected in the ledger as a reference for future transactions.

The *Guardian* has a short article that describes different places where Bitcoin is accepted as payment. *Bitcoin Magazine* also has a list of items by price range. Bitcoins can be used for Internet and mobile services, online products (e.g., games), physical products (e.g., electronics), and other professional services. Bitcoin has also come under scrutiny for its utility in purchasing illegal goods since using it provides a degree of anonymity. The most recent controversy was its use in the Silk Road, an online black market that was recently shut down by the FBI. Bitcoin ATMs are now appearing, which allow people to buy bitcoins at a physical ATM in their cities.

●●●

Bitcoin Basics

Bitcoin is a new kind of digital currency and payment network, first implemented in 2009.

It is a peer to peer, decentralized system, not run or managed by any national government, bank, or central authority.

All transactions are recorded on the **"block chain"** – a public ledger that each Bitcoin user accesses. It's used as a reference for all future transactions. The block chain is made out of many **blocks**, which you can imagine as pages in the ledger. Blocks also contain other data that is important for **"mining."**

The procedure of mining is used to process Bitcoin transactions.

Mining involves a computer solving a math problem that is found in each block. People who use their computers for mining are called **miners**.

Once a problem is solved, one block of bitcoins is added to the block chain (called producing or solving a block). Miners who solve the problems are rewarded with bitcoins. This is their incentive for lending their computer's processing power to mining.

The problems are adjusted over time for difficulty so that a new block is produced every 10 minutes.

Currently (March 2014), roughly 12.5 million bitcoins are in existence.

99% of all bitcoin will be by created by 2032. There will never be more than 21 million bitcoins.

Bitcoin users manage their bitcoins with free "wallet" software.

Wallets generate "addresses", which are like email addresses from which users can send and receive bitcoins. Addresses are a string of 27-34 alphanumeric characters.

Users can spend bitcoins at a number of online stores, and now, in growing numbers, physical locations.

Bitcoins can be bought and sold at online exchanges.

The value of Bitcoin (e.g., in US dollars) is determined by what people are willing to pay for it – there is no fixed value relative to other currencies.

The value of one bitcoin in US dollars was quite low from its debut in 2009 until April 2013 when it regularly was over $100, and then grew rapidly after November 2013, hitting a peak around $1200.

Bitcoin Advantages or Unique Features

- Little to no transaction fees**
- Bitcoin transactions are irreversible (they can only be refunded by users who receive funds)
- Anyone can send, receive, buy, or sell bitcoins
- Bitcoin transactions can be viewed using a block chain browser (the transactions do not contain personally identifiable information)

- Bitcoins can be sent anywhere in the world (across borders, countries) using the Internet
- Users do not need an account at any bank to use Bitcoin (although they'll likely need one to cash out their bitcoins for their country's currency)
- There is only a finite number of bitcoins created*
- There is no central authority governing or controlling Bitcoin (e.g., its value in USD)*
- Bitcoin is still experimental

*denotes more contentious issues

**somewhat complicated by mining - see Appendix A for more informations

3 - MAIN CHALLENGES TO BITCOIN OVERVIEW

There are several significant challenges to Bitcoin's survival and growth. The rest of the book will discuss these challenges and show possible responses to them. These challenges are interrelated but are discussed separately for convenience and ease of reading.

The first challenge is that of practical difficulty in using Bitcoin. This encompasses awareness, education, ease of use, and trust. It's the question of whether many people will be able to purchase and use Bitcoin at all in the way they use email, browse websites for leisure, go to the bank, buy things with their credit card, etc. It's also the question of whether retailers have incentives to use Bitcoin instead of other payment methods. The biggest difficulty in accepting it, however, is its current volatility.

Another challenge is the deflationary nature of Bitcoin. The criticism is that because Bitcoin has only a limited number of total bitcoins, the value of bitcoins will grow relative to a given basket of goods. There will not be enough bitcoins available for all the people who will want them, due to the fixed number of bitcoins, so their value will continue to grow. People will not spend their bitcoins now because their value will be higher in the future. This leads to a decline in consumption, a general decline in prices to entice spending, and dire economic consequences. Or so the line of thought goes. The consequences of the limited supply of bitcoins are one of the more debated features. The debate also involves conflicting views of the place of consumption, debt, and saving in today's economy.

The issue of holding on to bitcoins instead of spending them as their value appreciates is also tied to the question of saving or hoarding bitcoins. A related concern is whether a majority of bitcoins are currently held by few parties who are not spending them and have the ability to trigger large shifts in value by massive and rapid sell-offs.

The likelihood of governmental regulation and intervention that can control the use of Bitcoin is another significant challenge, for if the previous challenges have been overcome and Bitcoin grows in acceptance, governmental intervention will be inevitable and will effectively put an end to Bitcoin's future. Bitcoin is also vulnerable to something called a 51% attack - this attack might be paired with regulation or control efforts. The result in either case will mean a great disincentive for users to continue with Bitcoin. To circumvent regulation would require knowledge of the capabilities of the Internet and technical competency that is not commonly found.

While Bitcoin faces other challenges, these are the most significant and the most difficult to overcome.

4 - HURDLES TO ACCEPTANCE

The Challenge of Incentives

It's still questionable which incentives are significant enough for customers and merchants to use Bitcoin. Before I start, some supporters of Bitcoin will question the nature of the incentives we should be looking at. For if Bitcoin is viewed as much larger project in creating something such as an alternative economy at a large scale, then they might see the difficulties I'll show as mere growing pains that will be dealt with as time passes, adoption increases, and the collective knowledge of Bitcoin developers and enthusiasts improves. That objection will be dealt with at the end of this chapter as well as the next chapter. It is also very questionable when considering the possibility of regulation and control.

It is still important, however, to illustrate the currently existing practical difficulties that hamper Bitcoin adoption.

For customers, there's still little incentive when shopping domestically to use Bitcoin over other means of payment. Customers still have to jump through hoops to buy things with bitcoin in the first place, such as setting up a wallet, purchasing bitcoins at an exchange, and finding merchants who actually accept bitcoin. Of course, it can be said that using credit cards has its own hoops to jump through. But it can't be ignored how ingrained using credit cards is among customers. Convention and ease of use in the user experience is a very powerful force in shaping behavior.

It isn't a simple matter of education in persuading people to adopt Bitcoin. If that were the case, would previous digital currencies have all failed? It's not only showing a potential user the bare steps of setting up software and how to purchase and spend coins, as if inputting instructions to a machine. There's a whole way of thinking and a familiarity with a certain culture that's involved. Bitcoin users and technology enthusiasts take this knowledge for granted because they are at ease with all things technology and Internet related. Yes, perhaps a minority of people may become comfortable with using it, out of sheer force of individual will and interest, but it's not a realistic assumption to expect all consumers to jump on the Bitcoin bandwagon when the practical incentives to use it are still unclear.

Credit card use provides protections for fraud, chargebacks, warranty, among a number of other well-known benefits. But even if these were all shams, would that even change Bitcoin's marginal position? Again, convention and the value of many users already using it is no small matter (also called the network effects), and it's no small feat for it to be dislodged.

It has been suggested that people in the developing world may become Bitcoin's biggest users because Bitcoin will provide an easier means to purchase and sell goods than going through a bank where cash is the norm and infrastructure for credit cards is lacking. Counting on this is too speculative considering it's not even there at a nascent stage. Such an avenue is still little more than wishful proposals.

Volatility

The biggest hurdle for the wide adoption of Bitcoin, however, for both customers and merchants, is Bitcoin's volatility.

To take a recent example, between January 7 2014 and January 11 2014, Bitcoin's market price in US dollars has decreased $100 (approximately from $1000 to $900). That's a 10% decrease in roughly four days. Just say you bought one bitcoin on the 7th spending $1000 USD. Your bitcoin is now worth $100 USD less in four days.

One possibility to counter these kinds of losses is to only buy bitcoins at the moment when you know exactly when you are going to spend them. This can be done by keeping an amount of some other currency on one's online exchange account - something like a "quick conversion" fund. And perhaps other features or software will be developed to assist this kind of instantaneous conversion-purchase strategy. But it raises the question again if there's really anything worth purchasing using Bitcoin alone that would make one go down this path.

Let's consider the alternate scenario, where Bitcoin goes up in value. Between December 30, 2013, and January 7, 2014, one bitcoin grew from roughly $750 to $1000. So if you bought one bitcoin, you would have gained about $250 doing nothing other than buying it at the right time and holding on to it instead of spending it. Great, right? But the question becomes why would you ever spend your bitcoin if you thought its value was going to increase?

One reply from Bitcoin supporters is that you need or want to buy your good now. The weakness in this reply lies in the fact that for many customers there is no good that you can buy in bitcoin that you can't just buy using regular old dollars or using your credit card. You could hold on to your bitcoin while its value appreciates and just buy whatever you need using a different widely accepted currency. Then, you could sell your bitcoin to someone else when you felt you'd profit enough from selling it. The bitcoin therefore barely circulates.

Let's consider the volatility issue from the side of merchants now. If they priced something as 1 bitcoin, then received 1 bitcoin as payment, while the value of 1 bitcoin declines soon after, they have effectively lost money they could have gotten if they had just priced the good in USD. One way this possibly remedied is by using a service that converts the bitcoin to a currency such as USD immediately after the payment is received. But what's the point of this? It's just adding another layer to the transactions which has its own costs, although perhaps minimal (assuming a best case). Is there an immediately compelling financially beneficial reason for this to become widespread? It works around the volatility issue but seems needlessly complicated for people unless they are already convinced of the importance of using Bitcoin.

There have been suggestions that customers will spend bitcoin when merchants provide incentives of their own (e.g., offering discounts for customers who purchase in bitcoin). And perhaps there may be slight gains in popularity and notoriety for a business if it becomes known they are accepting bitcoin. But these are hardly guarantees of anything and are still individualistic rather than systemic in scope.

Much is made of the benefits of non-reversible transactions. Perhaps it can benefit merchants when it comes to avoiding fraudulent activity from customers. Yet for merchants too this is a questionable benefit, because what recourse will they have to their suppliers if the transactions are non-reversible?

Questionable Faith in Eventual Stability

It's sometimes asserted that Bitcoin will eventually no longer be volatile. It is said that once Bitcoin commands a sufficient market size and volume the price will be much more stable. These assertions are sometimes also supported with claims that volatility will reduce when exchanges are more robust, there is a futures market, and other predictions.

The problem with all such assertions is that they are tantamount to "Bitcoin will be successful when it becomes successful." To say that stability will be reached when many more people are using Bitcoin isn't an argument, but a prediction that already assumes its success. It already assumes that more and more people will become regular spenders, traders, or active users and followers of Bitcoin. But that's exactly what's in question. Imagine if someone were stating that he would become a famous actor. This person's argument is that he will become a successful actor once Hollywood agents notice him and cast him in increasingly significant films. But of course, this isn't an argument at all, and nothing logically follows from his current lack of fame. Unfortunately there are only predictions (greater number of participants, more movement of the currency, robust exchanges, etc.) in support of predictions (that the price will become stable). As an aside, gold, the commodity Bitcoin is often compared with, is still volatile.

But there are more fundamental problems that have been hinted at which will be covered in the next chapter and make stability seem unlikely. These are deflation and the concentration of bitcoin ownership.

5 - DEFLATION, HOARDING, AND THE CONCENTRATION OF OWNERSHIP

Recall that there is only a finite number of bitcoins that can be mined. Once these are mined, no new bitcoins will be in existence. Any bitcoins lost (e.g., if a wallet is lost) are removed out of circulation and remain dormant forever.

If the use of bitcoins becomes more widespread, there will be a greater demand for them as a medium of exchange and they will be increasing in value and as a means of investment. As they increase in value, people will hold on to their bitcoins instead of spending them. And as more people invest in bitcoins, their value will increase even more. That is, the rising demand for bitcoins causes the demand to rise even further. People will not spend their bitcoins because each bitcoin will be worth more and will have a higher purchasing power in the future. As no one is spending their bitcoins, producers reduce prices. This reduction in prices is called deflation. It is important to remember that the **average** price level decreases over time.

There are two big problems in such a scenario. The

problem isn't if only a few agents are refusing to spend their bitcoins. If there is **widespread** hoarding of bitcoins, people aren't buying things. If people aren't buying things, producers won't produce things and then won't pay workers. Circulation of bitcoins ends. Eventually a crash in the value results as people holding on to bitcoins realize their value as investments was only based on rising demand for the currency, that is, demand feeding the rise of demand alone. The value was based on an "irrational exuberance" rather than any fundamentals.

Another problem for deflation is how the uncertainty in long term prospects is manifested in contracts and debts. If someone is in debt 60 bitcoins because they took a loan, and their wages go down from 20 bitcoins to 10 bitcoins, the debt will become one sixth of his or her wages instead of one third and will be more difficult to repay. But the value of this person's regular payments to the lender would be increasing as per deflation. It's also questionable why loans would be given during the deflationary period. Simply holding on to the bitcoins would raise their value. Loaning them would not be required to gain value, especially considering that giving a loan has its own risk. Even if loans were given, it's too risky to take them out to start a new business because the debt will be harder to pay. In the end, Bitcoin is unsustainable as a currency.

The line of thinking above is decried as Keynesian propaganda by many believers in Bitcoin. They often give several general objections to the scenario. But none of them really work, or they all require an already established belief in Bitcoin's eventual success to work.

One objection is to deny that there will be a lack of spending when the value rises due to demand for bitcoins. This is said because people want and need goods now – they will not wait indefinitely as their currency increases in value or as prices decrease to spend and invest. The problem with this is that while it's true that certain things may need to be purchased, such as groceries or other necessities, many other purchases can still be delayed. Other more substantial purchases can be delayed as higher prices associated with them go down. This objection takes a particular consumer-centric perspective (i.e., "I want to buy the new video games now, not weeks later") and generalizes it to all spending. Other large investment projects do not succumb to the same "spend it now" logic since they involve considerably more risk and coordination.

The above objection seems contradictory in its philosophy to the objection that deflation is actually a good thing because it reduces consumerism. Perhaps more sustainable products will have to be created in the kind of deflationary period associated with Bitcoin. There are two main problems with this objection. The first is more pragmatic. Will business owners really want to participate in Bitcoin if they are told at the outset by Bitcoin evangelists that they are going to have to change their production to suit the environment that would be the result of widespread Bitcoin adoption? That they would have to produce less and make less money? The second problem is more fundamental. Without consumerism and constant consumption, how is growth in a capitalist system as we live in it today possible? Somewhat ironically, for this very reason Bitcoin has been supported by some anti-capitalists because of the lack of consumption that would occur during deflation.

Supporters also sometimes attempt to defuse the deflation problem in a similar manner with respect to the lack of consumption by stating that deflation encourages saving, and saving is a good thing. But bitcoins aren't being saved so that they can be used more productively by some other enterprises. That is, they aren't being invested. They are being hoarded. They are sitting in the digital equivalent of a sock under the bed. And the question still remains why they would even be invested so that a return can be made if simply holding them without activity still increases their value. Investing still involves risk. Similarly, if the investment were for an enterprise that led to the production of goods, who would spend their bitcoins on them, when they again could just wait as their value increases without activity?

There are also declamations that people will spend their bitcoins out of a sense of altruism or for the sake of seeing the community of Bitcoin users grow and thrive. Empirically this is false. The majority of bitcoins are not circulating (see Ron and Shamir's article, also summarized in Arstechnica). It also presupposes the success of Bitcoin, bypassing all the substantial obstacles in the way of it becoming widely accepted, not to mention the hazards of regulation.

Concentration of Ownership

927 people own half of all the bitcoins in existence. Another 10,000 own another quarter. The rest of the users, more than one million of them, only own less than a quarter put together.

There is a great risk in having a very small group of people control such a large supply of bitcoins. This a potential risk because this group may crash the market for their own profits (such as in a pump and dump scenario). And why assume any altruistic motivations on their parts? Why would they spend the coins to facilitate the growth of the Bitcoin economy?

Sometimes this is countered by suggesting that currencies today also have this degree of control by a number of certain groups or powers. But how can this be interpreted in any way as a positive feature for Bitcoin? Perhaps it might be argued that this state of affairs is unavoidable, or that it is the natural result of those early adopters of Bitcoin who mined many coins. But why would anyone who isn't already a believer in Bitcoin be anything but extremely hesitant to get involved in a currency that's so unequally distributed? Sometimes this is justified by saying that early adopters took risk in mining or participating in the Bitcoin project at the beginning. Let's assume that's true. The problem is then why should anyone from the outside care about that, if the fact is right now it seems that stepping into such a scenario seems unnecessarily risky?

6 - REGULATION AND CONTROL

Regulation and control provide a significant challenge to the growth and survival of Bitcoin. I don't want to get into the details of the currently existing regulations limiting the use of Bitcoin to determine an exact interpretation of its current standing. I think that is really beside the point and to extrapolate from any openings or warm receptions in some countries to a prosperous future for Bitcoin is misguided. The legal status of Bitcoin has its own Wikipedia page summarizing the laws involving Bitcoin activity in two dozen countries (as of March 2014) for your own reference. Countries with stronger stances or regulations against Bitcoin are Iceland, India, Indonesia, Taiwan, and Russia. But what's more important to consider is whether it's likely Bitcoin's downfall can be caused by regulation and control.

There are two broad questions to be considered. The first is whether nation states will regulate or control Bitcoin. The second is whether they can feasibly regulate and control it. I believe both are near certainties.

This regulation and control can take different forms. Recently in Thailand, there was an outright ban on Bitcoin activities. It was illegal to "buy and sell Bitcoins, buy or sell any goods or services in exchange for Bitcoins, send any Bitcoins to anyone outside of Thailand, or receive Bitcoins from anyone outside the country" (The *Telegraph* – "Bitcoins banned in Thailand"). Foreign exchange trading with Bitcoin is illegal in Iceland. Bitcoin ATMs cannot be installed in Taiwan because the country's Financial Supervisory Commission believes Bitcoin is not a currency and should not be accepted by individuals or banks as payment. Among other countries there are concerns about Bitcoin's use for illegal transactions in drugs and child pornography as well as its role in tax evasion.

As I have shown previously, there are already significant challenges in the way of Bitcoin's wide acceptance. But assume somehow those challenges are overcome even though they seem inherent to Bitcoin's very existence. If Bitcoin then becomes more widely accepted and used, it is certain it will face regulation and control.

That is because it effectively creates an alternative economy within each nation. Bitcoins circulate and circumvent the state's financial institutions. This is an abstract scenario, of course. Yet even this scenario is not necessary for Bitcoin to face increased significant regulation. We can easily imagine a situation where Bitcoin's involvement in the funding of some kind of high profile act (drugs, prostitution, terrorism) leads to fervent calls for its control. What's more is that it doesn't even have to be truly involved, as long as it is negatively implicated.

Assume it is made illegal in a nation. What actions might actually be taken by governments and institutions to prevent Bitcoin's use and growth? Would that even be necessary, if the news causes a crash in the value? Attacking individual users would be too time consuming. But they can pursue online and physical exchanges, which would make it difficult for anyone to buy and sell their Bitcoins. Notable marketplaces and vendors that accept

Bitcoin for their products may be commanded to prohibit transactions in Bitcoin.

Here supporters of Bitcoin may sometimes argue that Bitcoin can still thrive because of its decentralized nature (there is no "center" to target and remove) as well as the limitations of all regulatory efforts. Activities will move to black markets to avoid detection and control. The existence of movie or music sharing or torrenting sites such as The Pirate Bay is also used as evidence against the strength of the regulatory powers of institutions in a cyber-environment.

But if Bitcoin moves exclusively to black markets, it is doubtful that anyone outside the most faithful believers in Bitcoin or users who want goods that are only available on the black market will still use it. Who will use Bitcoin if most vendors can't legally accept it as payment? Again, it is likely that there will be black markets, but it is hard to imagine more than a minority of people using them, just so that they can use their bitcoins. Not to mention the knowledge hurdles involved in being confident using these black markets. I also think it's disingenuous to compare torrenting sites to Bitcoin exchanges and markets, because as I said earlier, an alternative currency means an alternative economy and is a challenge to a state's sovereignty and monetary policy. That seems a more serious threat to a state than file sharing. This was recognized back in 2003 in economist Robert Guttmann's book, *Cybercash*, where he noted free market supporters' reception of electronic money as a "private money form capable of escaping government regulation quite effectively", something capable of "disassociation from government control" (Guttmann, 89). Yet if it is effectively used underground, might it then resurge again in popularity? But then it would be more obvious as a target if it did significantly grow.

The FBI in late 2013 had shut down the Silk Road, a popular black market exchange where users could trade illicit goods for Bitcoins. The CEO of BitInstant, a Bitcoin exchange, was arrested and charged with money laundering in January 2014. Of course, perhaps other exchanges may not be taken down as easily as this one was. And others will certainly replace it. But would that matter for the future for most users? Would there be enough users and vendors still strong enough believers in the worth of the currency after they witness large scale seizures? And would they want to be associated with that 'scene', however accurate or inaccurate the reputation is? Not to mention the difficulties for users to convert their bitcoins into cash from banks, as Canadian banks have shut down accounts owned by Canadian companies who trade bitcoins and convert it into cash for consumers (see *Global News* article). Another possibility institutions may use is the 51% attack, which is explained in the next chapter.

What if major corporations associate themselves with Bitcoin? This seems unlikely, given what I have discussed previously. Any association would also seem to be based on a short term or speculation basis, rather than any long term faith in the project. But assume there is some association. Would this perhaps increase Bitcoin's chance of survival? It was suggested that Bitcoin is moving toward integration with traditional services in a January 30th 2014 article in *Fortune*. An attorney quoted in the article expresses his view that in the face of regulation, "[Bitcoin service development] will shift to other jurisdictions, taking jobs and the resulting wealth with it. The true losers will be U.S. residents."

Such an association seems doubtful (unlikely as it is ever to happen) because of the regulation that would be involved that would steer the user base away. How could states allow the volumes of Bitcoin associated with a major party's sponsorship go unregulated? In such a scenario, it is hard to imagine anonymity and privacy being considered a priority, as there would have to be the maintenance of proper records, the reporting of currency transactions that are over a certain dollar value or involve illegal use, and other requirements. This is not a viable option since the appeal of Bitcoin is avoiding this kind of centralized control, monitoring, and authority.

Another possibility, equally dismal for most average users of Bitcoin, is that powerful institutions such as major banks or other large investors would be able to use Bitcoin more comfortably in the face of regulation, given their advantages in knowledge and information gathering and their relationships with powerful groups, including governments. I think this outcome is unlikely, but either way I don't think the average user or vendor of Bitcoin will stand to benefit.

Wishful Outcomes

It's sometimes said that people will be enraged by news of Bitcoin's control and regulation. They will then be even more committed to ensuring its survival.

It's also sometimes said that central banks or other institutions should not inhibit Bitcoin's development. (However, some Bitcoin supporters do not believe in that, rejecting the premise that certain institutions will have powers to control it, because they wish to totally work outside of the system).

By now I think it is clear these are not believable outcomes. The first already implies the success of Bitcoin in a wide or powerful base of support who would continue to use it instead of cashing out. But this is precisely what is in doubt.

The second also seems to miss what Bitcoin could be capable of in a highly idealistic scenario. Seeking approval from a national source seems fundamentally confused since Bitcoin would represent a threat to sovereignty and monetary policy.

7 - THE 51% ATTACK

In January 2014, Bitcoin almost experienced a 51% attack as the mining pool "Ghash.io" was close to comprising the majority hashrate of the network. Hashrate is a measuring unit of the processing power of the Bitcoin network. It's an estimation of the ability to solve the math problems in mining (that is, the ability to process hashes - see Appendix A). In a 51% attack, an attacker or group that has more than 50% of the network's processing power uses their power to control transactions. They could prevent transactions or new blocks from being accepted, which would stop payments and shut down the network. If they didn't want to take down the entire network, they could also double-spend coins. Bitcoin goes with the longest chain for future transactions, and this is where the attack's power comes in. There might be a number of chains at one time. But the attackers can create a chain that is longer. They can do this because they generate blocks faster than the rest of the network, so they create a branch off the main branch built by the network and work on extending it. "Longer chain" has a slightly different meaning here – it means the chain with the most combined difficulty (see the appendix "What is Mining" for more explanation).

In June 2013, a different digital currency called Feathercoin experienced a 51% attack. Feathercoin is still being used today, however.

In the Ghash.io case, the immediate threat was resolved by people leaving the Ghash.io mining pool. But the 51% attack is still a topic of concern considering the distribution of the market share of popular Bitcoin mining pools, where 3 mining pools put together have more than 50% of the hashrate distribution. This has varied recently and may continue to vary. But this seems concerning if the Bitcoin mining economy goes down the expected road of greater concentration of power and wealth over time. I don't think calls for altruism or ethical guidelines for mining will be effective at any point to stop it.

There is no reliable decentralized solution to a 51% attack. The only defenses are practical difficulties standing in its way. One is the cost to afford the computing power to be able to carry it out. But this number, however large, really is negligible to any developed country's institutional power or finances. Another objection is that such an attack would be unprofitable. But this objection assumes a financial goal, rather than various strategic goals. It doesn't matter if the user base is decentralized, if mining is controlled.

8 - CONCLUSION

Summary of Arguments

Bitcoin still has a usability hurdle. But even if that is overcome, Bitcoin's volatility makes it unlikely to reach wide acceptance. If it's not used by vendors, its use is limited.

It also faces strong long-term challenges in the way of deflation.

There is also a risk in the distribution of bitcoin ownership.

Even if it somehow surmounts those difficulties, it is still likely to be regulated and controlled by governments and other powerful institutions, effectively stopping its popular adoption. Different methods may be used, such as targeting exchanges, bank regulation to hamper cashing out of bitcoins, media efforts, or a 51% attack. If this has the effect of driving Bitcoin underground, adoption will be limited. One, because growth out of those underground channels will draw attention, and two, because the number of people who are tech savvy enough to feel confident in navigating those channels is a minority of the population.

So When Might You Use Bitcoin?

If you really believe in the project and what it represents, then perhaps you will feel compelled to become a user. Another reason is to use it as a speculative asset, looking for short term gains. But there are a number of things you should be confident in navigating in that case, such as finding reliable exchanges, knowing how to get the highest value for your bitcoins, and knowing how you can easily cash out, since this is becoming more controlled. If you are operating your business perhaps you might only accept them if you or someone else you work with is confident in selling the bitcoins you earn for profit. I have not yet researched any tangible benefits obtained through publicity by stating a vendor's bitcoin acceptance. Another option is just to use Bitcoin as a payment transfer system, not really considering it as a currency with long term value. For example, you want to send someone the value of $1000 USD in bitcoins right now, but for whatever reason, you don't have other options.

The Philosophies of Bitcoin

It is topic unto itself, but it is also questionable if Bitcoin can be separated from other political philosophies and economic systems. Currently, Bitcoin, if it is ever associated with any philosophies or schools of thought, is most often associated with American style libertarianism, anarcho-capitalism, and Austrian economics. However, there are other users who only are interested in Bitcoin as a payment transfer system alone. It is also associated with philosophies influenced by the power and potential of technology, such as cyber-utopianism or cryptoanarchism. In my opinion, it cannot be separated from the philosophies, at least in theory. The economic arguments (especially defending deflation) draw from Austrian economics. The justifications for decentralization and the arguments against centralization are put in American style libertarianism and anarcho-capitalism terms. The view is that the market's machinations are not to be tampered with and lead to better outcomes overall – but if they do not (say in cases of disparities in wealth), it is unjustifiable to interfere, politically or ethically. There is disagreement over the current divisions of wealth and the role nation states and its institutions play in skewing outcomes. In contrast, Bitcoin represents a purer system, again, at least in theory. Ignoring the obvious context Bitcoin is part of where economic power is quite concentrated seems to me to be a major blind spot for many supporters. What reason is there to believe Bitcoin, if it did represent a nobler ideal that has since been deviated from or not yet achieved, would not be coopted by that power? Strange justifications are used for effects of powerful agents participating, such as those arguing in favor of speculation because it will eventually lead to a state of equilibrium. Here I think the political ideal overtakes the mundane reality. Does Bitcoin's success require political and philosophical buy-in on a wide scale? If that is the case, success seems extremely unlikely. Does Bitcoin require high-profile evangelists or a kind of 'vanguard party' to further its position? As I have suggested, I think that will actually backfire against the purer theoretical ideals of Bitcoin, leading either to Bitcoin's destruction or neutralization via cooption from the powers that be. This is not an emotive or ethical claim for or against such a state of affairs, but a mere logical prediction

Common Themes and Concluding Thoughts

I think there is an interesting irony in the challenges Bitcoin faces. Decentralization was an important initial feature. Yet the power in mining and bitcoin ownership is quite concentrated. Was this something unavoidable in a capitalist world where economic power is also quite concentrated?

There is also debate about whether Bitcoin has focused

too much on technical solutions for social problems. Some people even question whether such distinctions can be made. But I think it is a valuable distinction. The challenges I have shown in this book are not particular to any technology. These are all inherent in any system in our society. The concentration of power, whether it is economic or social, if you think it is a good or bad thing, is a reality today that has many consequences that limits how far alternative movements may go. Some of the challenges have been recognized for a long time. The essence of the 51% attack is found in Plato's *Republic*, written more than 2000 years ago. Alternative movements have been crushed many times in the past. Our own optimism about various movements should always be tempered by the realization that others are as optimistic about their own movements, and this should give us pause to consider what challenges we are really facing.

A more cynical observer might suggest that Bitcoin was a doomed idea from the start because of the drive to locate trust away from social contexts into an objective technological one. Recall the 2008 paper by Nakamoto, describing "a system for electronic transactions without relying on trust." Only time will tell whether Bitcoin will survive. As can be surmised from my arguments, I don't think it will survive very long. Other digital currencies may replace it. Yet I think they will face the same social challenges even if the technology is improved, namely of the knowledge required for a majority of people to comfortably use it, as well as the threat of regulation. Technology can always be improved, but it's the issues surrounding the users, the social actors of Bitcoin, that are most important, because without them, Bitcoin is nothing but an interesting new development in computer science. Without the users it is without life and consequence.

APPENDIX A - SUPPLEMENTARY EXPLANATION OF MINING

Before elaborating on what mining involves, it's necessary to introduce hash functions. Bitcoin uses one hash function named SHA-256.

Hash Functions

A hash function is an algorithm (a stepwise procedure) that takes the input of data of arbitrary length, and outputs it as fixed-length data. No matter the input, whether it's one character or one million characters, or any data at all really, the output of the hash will always be the same length. The input of the hash function is called the message, and the output of the hash is called the digest. The fixed-length output allows the digest to be significantly smaller than the input.

Let's look at some examples using the SHA-256 cryptographic hash function. It is a cryptographic hash function because it has certain properties that make it suitable for secure uses.

Let's use the novel written by Charles Dickens, "A Tale

of Two Cities", to try out the hash function. For the first example, let's use the famous opening phrase of the novel, "It was the best of times, it was the worst of times" as our input. Inputting that into the hash function gives us the digest:
"47b4196caffbd11a2df80881d457bd3f4acf3814c543aafb4e 624bd9369a1799". This digest is a hexadecimal expression (a numeral system using 0-9 and A-F to represent values) of a 256 bit output. Bits are a measurement of computer information. 256 bit output can make very large numbers - it can be up to 2 to the power of 256. If you're wondering how we got from the opening phrase to that hexadecimal expression, the answer is basically a lot of mathematics (see end of chapter for an explanatory link).

But if we change just one character from our example, the digest completely changes. Let's change the word "worst" to "blurst" so our new input is the silly sounding "It was the best of times, it was the blurst of times". In this case, when we calculate the hash function, the digest is "9ce0c2131d4cf739f1ef1446da3f93166bc24e2495e9de303a 98b0649ebeb3ca". We changed a few characters there, but if we changed even one, the entire output would be completely different.

That might have seemed totally pointless. But the hash function can be used to give a digest for larger data. I'm going to input my version of the novel. It's around 140,000 words. The output is
"195c2fd0b1bba68ec736937460716e55a46c0f03f317251ba e323f4908157fc4". So those 64 characters alone in hexadecimal are a unique digest of all the words in the novel. And if I make a minor change again, changing that famous phrase to our silly example, while keeping everything else the same, the output is "daba933f8c5d220a712b3ce2d08726ddb19ed7a1fc9bdb8f6 b314094aa839f0a". So making a minor change in the output changed the whole digest. It's completely different. No matter the length of the input, the length of the output

(the digest) will be the same. Also, no matter the length or arrangement of data for the input, no two messages will have the same digest. This is called collision resistance and is an important feature of cryptographic hash functions.

However, the same input always gives the same result. No matter how many times you use "It was the best of times, it was the worst of times" as your input, the output will be the same each time. Although these examples aren't very scientific and take a lot of liberties, essentially you now understand what a hash produces (there were some other topics like character encoding and binary representations not touched upon).

One modification of the input changed the entire output. As the outputs are so different each time, it's impossible to guess or predict what they will be based on the inputs – an important feature of a cryptographic has function. The hash function has to be calculated each time the input changes to determine what the output is. There's no way around it. This allows for "proof of work". The resulting output is "proof" that the "work" of calculating the digest from the message has been done. Someone also can't work backwards from the output to guess what the input was.

What This Has to Do with Mining

Going back to the analogy of the block chain being like a publicly viewable ledger book, I suggested seeing each page in the ledger as a block.

In each block, there's a variety of information. The body of the block contains the transactions.

Miners work with the header of the block. The header contains information such as a current timestamp. It also contains a hash of the transactions in the block. You can think of it kind of as a condensed number that uniquely summarizes all the transactions. Also in the header is a version number of the Bitcoin protocol being used and the miner's address so that they can get the bitcoin reward if they are successful.

The header also contains a number called "the target", as well as a number called the "nonce." There is also a hash of the previous block in the header. See all the information I've written about in the last two paragraphs? All that stuff is put into the hash function as the input, and the output is the hash of the block. If that is too confusing, just think back to the A Tale of Two Cities example I gave where I inputted the entire text of the novel. A bunch of information is being sent through the hash function as input to give a fixed length output.

Now, those digests, or outputs from the hash, are an alternative notation for very large numbers. The target (that number contained in the block header) is also a large number.

Miners take the block header as their input for the hash. They get an output from that process. That output is a large number. Their goal is to make the resulting number (that is, the output from the hash) smaller than the number of the "target."

Here is the catch. Remember how the same input will always give the same output for the hash function? So if the miner calculates the hash, and the output is higher than the target number, that same input that was used will always give that number. This is where the "nonce" comes in.

Remember how one change in the input for the hash function – any change at all – completely changes the output? Think back to the first two examples. Just changing one word completely changed the output from the hash function. That is, it gave a totally different number.

This is where the nonce comes in. The nonce is just a number in the header of the block that can be changed each time. Miners can start it at "0", and increase it each time they calculate the output. This allows the output from the hash to be different each time. That is because the input for the hash function is changing each time the nonce changes. And therefore, this gives miners the ability to try to eventually get under the target number. These calculations are all done very rapidly and with constantly updated information through Bitcoin software. Once the output number from the hash calculation is lower than the target number, that hash is sent to other miners whose computers verify if it works, and then relayed around the entire network. Basically, the block is created and is added to the block chain. Each block references the previous block. This reference is found in the block header. The block header contains a hash of the previous block header.

As an incentive for carrying out this whole process, miners are rewarded with new bitcoins if they create a block. This is through a special transaction included which is the block reward. This reward is paid to an address the miner gives. In addition to the block reward, miners earn transaction fees submitted for the block. While the transaction fee for each transaction may be very small, all of the transaction fees in one block are added together, giving another incentive for miners.

The block chain prevents double spending. Double spending is the result of spending the same digital token more than once, as in the case of someone sending the same bitcoin to two different places at the same time. It is considered a risk because digital information is reproduced relatively easily.

When a block is a created, transactions inside that block are said to be confirmed. When another block is created, the number of confirmations is increased by one. Waiting for 6 confirmations is usually recommended to prevent double spending. Six confirmations are recommended because the computing power required to carry out double spending at that point would unlikely be controlled by attackers. Conflicting transactions (one where the same bitcoin is spent in two different places at once) can't be in the blockchain, since having both transactions in the same block would make the block invalid – it would not be generated. A transaction would also be rejected if it rejected a transaction already included in a block that was already generated.

Each block confirms the previous block. Extreme computing power would be required to modify a block once multiple blocks have been generated after it, that is, after it had been confirmed multiple times. That is because every block after it would have to be created again. So if you have blocks 1, 2, 3, and 1 is modified, block 2 would have to be regenerated because it references block 1, and block 3 would have to be regenerated since it references block 2 (which references block 1). But if the extreme computing power is obtained, double spending is possible. For more information on this, see the 51% attack chapter.

The difficulty (a measure of how difficult it is to find a correct hash for a block – i.e., a hash below a given target) changes every 2016 blocks. Difficulty is the largest possible target (around 2 to the power of 224) divided by the current target. A link to the current target is included in this chapter's references page (it will be in hexadecimal).

Transaction Fees

Users can include fees for miners in their transactions so that miners would have more of an incentive to include them in their block. Miners can choose which transactions they want to include in the block they are trying to create. These transaction fees will become more important as the reward for mining decreases over time.

Topics Omitted from This Section

The explanation just given will suffice for the other chapters in this book and most of the Bitcoin related stories you will encounter day-to-day. I didn't focus on confirmation times for transactions or the finer details of mining and transaction fees. But these topics will now be more accessible to you via the other sources available on Bitcoin. If you are mathematically inclined you can read the different publications about SHA-256 and related cryptographic hash functions that are linked on the Wikipedia article http://en.wikipedia.org/wiki/SHA-2#External_links

TOPICS OMITTED

It's impossible to cover everything about Bitcoin in this kind of introductory book. Some topics I didn't cover are the role of public-key cryptography (especially as it relates to addresses), confirmation times, and the possible problems involving transaction fees and future incentives for miners. Another interesting issue is how anonymous Bitcoin is. However, I didn't examine it because I follow the argument that anonymity wasn't the main focus of the Bitcoin project. There are also other challenges Bitcoin faces such as Internet dependency or unregulated exchanges, but I don't think they are as critical as the ones discussed in this book. Some are also more technically focused than I think readers of this book would be inclined to read about for their initial foray into Bitcoin. These include the tracing of coin history, packet sniffing, and denial of service attacks.

FURTHER READING OR INFORMATION

If you are interested in learning more about cryptography, check out Khan Academy's introductory video series available to watch on Youtube:
https://www.khanacademy.org/math/applied-math/cryptography/crypt/v/intro-to-cryptography

Bitcoin is one of a number of cryptocurrencies, although it is the most popular at the moment. A cryptocurrency is a digital medium of exchange that incorporates cryptography to implement a secure information economy. You can find more information about the other cryptocurrencies on their Wikipedia article: http://en.wikipedia.org/wiki/Cryptocurrency.

The economist Paul Krugman is one notable critic of Bitcoin. His criticisms are the most well-known and focus on the deflation issue. His articles have generated a variety of responses. Some see his criticisms as common explications of Bitcoin's weak points, others see them as apologetics for state intervention. The divide has as much to do with philosophy as it does with economics.

REFERENCES

WHAT ARE BITCOINS AND WHY SHOULD I USE THEM?

Bitcoin Magazine. "Where to spend your bitcoins."
www.bitcoinmagazine.com/2651/where-to-spend-your-bitcoins/. October 25, 2012.

Blockchain.info. "Bitcoin Charts."
https://blockchain.info/charts. January 20, 2014.

BBC News (Leo Kelion). "Bitcoin sinks after China restricts yuan exchanges."
http://www.bbc.co.uk/news/technology-25428866.
December 18, 2013.

Forbes (Kelly Phillips Erb). "The End Of The (Silk) Road For Bitcoin Millionaire As IRS, Fed Agencies Make Arrests."
http://www.forbes.com/sites/kellyphillipserb/2014/02/01/the-end-of-the-silk-road-for-bitcoin-millionaire-as-irs-fed-agencies-make-arrests/.
February 1, 2014.

Satoshi Nakamoto. "Bitcoin: A Peer-to-Peer Electronic Cash System." https://bitcoin.org/bitcoin.pdf. 2008.

The Guardian. "Where can you use bitcoins a brief guide." http://www.theguardian.com/technology/2013/nov/25/where-can-you-use-bitcoins-brief-guide. November 25, 2013.

DEFLATION, HOARDING, AND THE CONCENTRATION OF OWNERSHIP

Ars Technica (Dan Goodin). "78 percent of Bitcoin currency stashed under digital mattress, study finds." http://arstechnica.com/tech-policy/2012/10/78-percent-of-bitcoin-currency-stashed-under-digital-mattress-study-finds/. October 17, 2012.

Business Insider (Rob Wile). "927 People Own Half Of All Bitcoins." http://www.businessinsider.com/927-people-own-half-of-the-bitcoins-2013-12. December 12, 2013.

CNET (Steven Musil). "Silk Road forfeits $28M in Bitcoins seized from its servers." http://news.cnet.com/8301-1023_3-57617393-93/silk-road-forfeits-$28m-in-bitcoins-seized-from-its-servers/. January 16, 2014.

Dorit Ron and Adi Shamir. "Quantitative Analysis of the Full Bitcoin Transaction Graph." http://eprint.iacr.org/2012/584.pdf. 2012.

Naked Capitalism (Lambert Strether). "Everything I was Afraid to Ask about Bitcoin but Did." http://www.nakedcapitalism.com/2013/11/everything-i-was-afraid-to-ask-about-bitcoin-but-did.html. November 21, 2013.

New Economic Perspectives (Dan Kervick). "Bitcoin's Deflationary Weirdness." http://neweconomicperspectives.org/2013/04/talking-bitcoin.html. April 24, 2013.

Wired (Cade Metz). "Bitcoin Is Flawed, But It Will Still Take Over the World." http://www.wired.com/wiredenterprise/2013/11/bitcoin-and-deflation/2/. November 25, 2013.

REGULATION AND CONTROL

Business Insider (Rob Wile). "CEO Of Bitcoin Exchange Arrested." http://www.businessinsider.com/report-ceo-of-major-bitcoin-exchange-arrested-2014-1. January 27, 2014.

CNN Money (David Z. Morris). "Bitcoin gets two hearings - and steps closer to acceptance." http://finance.fortune.cnn.com/2014/01/30/bitcoin-hearings-wells-fargo/. January 30, 2014.

Forbes (Andy Greenberg). "Silk Road Competitor Shuts Down And Another Plans To Go Offline After Claimed $6 Million Theft." http://www.forbes.com/sites/andygreenberg/2013/12/01/silk-road-competitor-shuts-down-and-another-plans-to-go-offline-after-6-million-theft/. December 1, 2013.

Forbes (Kelly Phillips Erb). "The End Of The (Silk) Road For Bitcoin Millionaire As IRS, Fed Agencies Make Arrests." http://www.forbes.com/sites/kellyphillipserb/2014/02/01/the-end-of-the-silk-road-for-bitcoin-millionaire-as-irs-fed-agencies-make-arrests/. February 1, 2014.

Global News (Jamie Sturgeon). "As Bitcoin surges, Canadian banks make converting to cash difficult." http://globalnews.ca/news/996853/as-bitcoin-surges-canadian-banks-make-converting-to-cash-difficult/. November 30, 2013.

Robert Guttmann. "Cybercash: The Coming Era of Electronic Money." Palgrave Macmillan, 2003. P. 89. http://us.macmillan.com/cybercash/RobertGuttmann.

TechCrunch (Catherine Shu). "Taiwan's Government Says No To Bitcoin ATMs." http://techcrunch.com/2014/01/05/taiwans-government-says-no-to-bitcoin-atms/. January 5, 2014.

Wikipedia. "Legal status of Bitcoin." http://en.wikipedia.org/wiki/Legal_status_of_Bitcoin.

THE 51% ATTACK

Blockchain.Info. "Bitcoin Hashrate Distribution." https://blockchain.info/pools.

Heavy (Danny Vega). "Ghash.io Nearly Ruins Bitcoin: 5 Fast Facts You Need to Know." http://www.heavy.com/tech/2014/01/ghash-io-51-percent-attack-bitcoin/. January 9, 2014.

APPENDIX A - SUPPLEMENTARY EXPLANATION OF MINING

Bitcoin Stack Exchange. "What are bitcoin miners really solving?" http://bitcoin.stackexchange.com/questions/8031/what-are-bitcoin-miners-really-solving February 28, 2013.

External Links to Government Publications on SHA-2, http://en.wikipedia.org/wiki/SHA-2#External_links.

Links to the target and other stats.
www.blockexplorer.com/q.

ABOUT THE AUTHOR

Marc is a writer interested in making contemporary ideas, debates, and technologies accessible to everyone.

You can find his blog at http://marcnovus.tumblr.com/. You can write in questions, comments, or suggest future topics for him to cover.

You can also follow him on Twitter at https://twitter.com/marcnovus

NOTES

www.ingramcontent.com/pod-product-compliance
Lightning Source LLC
Chambersburg PA
CBHW020709180526
45163CB00008B/3011